Unknown

TECNO W2

1

TABLE OF CONTENTS

CHAPTER

3. Step #1: Pick The Right Songs

-Go Easy

-A "Signature Song"

4. Step #2: Choose The Right Audience

-Know Your Audience

-Build A Good Audience

-Be A Good Audience Member

5. Step #3: Rehearse Your Songs

-Prepare Yourself

-Don't Forget The Lyrics

-Start With A Warmup

-Ask A Friend

6. Step #4: Dress Up For The Show

PART ONE
WHAT YOU NEED TO KNOW

CHAPTER 1

DON'T SING THE "I SUCK" SONG

"I SUCK at karaoke" "I get nervous everytime" OR even "They just don't like my singing" Is this the song you're singing? Is this how you feel about your singing and particularly, karaoke? Or perhaps you haven't found the courage to give stage-singing a shot, or you think you don't have what it takes to pull it off?

I know the Feeling

Well you're not alone, I sometimes get nervous too, before going on stage and quite frankly, I really didn't like my singing at some time in my life. I still don't... Maybe I do sometimes... okay all the time :D

You get better with time as you practice. I have, and you have to believe that you can too.

And while I can't say I'm a professional at singing, I can say I'm a good singer... in the bathroom especially. Lol!

So just how do they -the really good singers- do it? Hmmm!

CHAPTER 2

THE PLAIN TRUTH

Apparently, people who do better at singing have better luck because they're just born that way right? Uh! Wrong!

We've all had some of those times in our lives when we sucked at something -including singing karaoke. Sometimes due to a lot of tension on our part, which is quite normal. Other times due to other factors like poor singing practices, techniques and all of that stuff.

Being nervous can be a good Sign

Truth is we all want to have a great performance and put up a great show, but then we let those 'nerves' override us, causing us to shut down or underperform.

We somehow feel that the fact that we are nervous means something's not right, but even great performers get nervous. But being nervous doesn't have to be such a bad thing.

Like famous performer, James Corden says "I think you're only ever nervous if you want to do your best."

And it makes sense because, if doing a great job at something wasn't important to you, you probably wouldn't care or be nerved up about it. So yes, it is okay to be nervous. It shows you really want to do a good job at singing.

Being nervous while singing isn't helpful though.

Don't be hard on Yourself

If you think people just don't like your singing, it's probably because they(not all of them) actually don't like your singing. Some people can be tough to please, even by professional singers. Don't be hard on yourself. You can be better.

Take singing lessons. Invest in vocal training if necessary. Start witha *karaoke box* if possible with just friends and probably a few other persons so you're more relaxed. Ask a better singer-friend to help you out with your singing too.

And if you already have been on stage before, enjoy your singing more. Take a compliment given to you when you do a good job and if you don't put up a good performance, don't give up. Try again!

Enjoy yourself while you sing even if you're new to this whole singing-in-public thingy. Just take one step at a time. You'll get to where you dream of being, eventually.

One step at a Time

Now this book may not make you a great la-la-la-ing Opera Singer, but it sure will show you what you need to do to be better at singing karaoke when you go out this weekend, plus how you can go about it.

There are some steps you could take to help you get started on your path to a better karaoke or even a great singing career. These steps should help keep "suck" at bay and let you have a blast singing karaoke even if you're new to this, and we'll be looking at those steps in a bit.

You can have a better karaoke performance. Yes you can! You can do this if you believe you can. This could be the start of something big. Are you ready for this? **Let's go!**

PART TWO

THE STEPS - YOUR PREPARATION

CHAPTER 3

STEP #1: PICK THE RIGHT SONGS

Picking the right song for your karaoke performance is very important as it can help you better your performance even if you were setup by your crazy friends to do a song at the last minute ;P

Go Easy

So when picking songs, you want to pick about 2 or 3 songs that are simple, and that you can sing easily, and then rehearse any of them, to perform on the day of your performance.

Don't go for songs with much vocal technicality, especially if you're a newbie to this.

Pick a song with a *vocal range* that you can sing quite well, and that you probably, not compulsorily, have sang in the shower like a thousand times already.

Stick to an easy song. I mean we all love Adele, but a "Hello from the other side" can wait. ;D

A "Signature Song"

The song you pick should be capable of "carrying your audience along." One easy way to go about this is to consider choosing a "Signature Song" This is simply a well-known song which your audience can easily connect with, but make sure it's a song you know quite well too.

Don't pick songs that give your audience a hard time singing or one they've never heard of.

Pick a song that your audience can join in easily or chorus back while you sing. After all, they are there to have a good time just like you. Give them a good time.

Also you can choose a song that you have an emotional connection with. If you've got a song well within your vocal range, that you love so much and you have an attachment to, go for it.

You could also consider picking a song based on the kind of audience you're singing to. You can skip this process though, but just for cautions sake, you can carry it out. For instance, picking a "John Legend" song to perform to a crowd of mainly "Pasuma" music lovers doesn't really add up. So to be on a safer side, you can consider this measure.

You can pick a song that most likely than not, would appeal to that particular audience, but ensure you're familiar with the lyrics.

Picking the right song can be the difference between a good performance and a not-so-good one, so ensure you do this. It will make a difference.

Note: There are other factors that influence what type of song would be right for you like voice texture, vocal range and type of voice. One reason why you should consider investing in a voice coach.

CHAPTER 4

STEP #2: CHOOSE THE RIGHT AUDIENCE

This may seem irrelevant, but it's quite important. Probably one the most important steps you need to take in having a better karaoke. Just like you would want to pick a good song to perform, you also want to pick a good audience to listen to it. The right audience.

Know your Audience

First of all, you want an audience that is obviously interested in good music and cheer people whenever they sing well, as well as an audience that would be receptive to whichever song you eventually go for.

Okay, apparently such an audience doesn't exist. Everyone can not love your singing, or even a particular song, but you need to be sure they are an interesting audience. In other words "Know Your Audience."

Say you go visiting a friend of yours in another State, or you're on your *NYSC* (National Youth Service Corps), and you want to go sing karaoke at a bar near you. You should consider knowing the area.

What kind of area it is, where the bar is located. What type of music would people in such an area be receptive to. Which popular music artist is from such an area or celebrated more there.

Little things like these can add points to acing your karaoke performance. This doesn't guarantee a flawless performance, but it would go a long way if you do it.

Everyone connects with different types of music though, but you want to be sure you get to know your audience a little bit.

Build a good Audience

Also go with some friends to your karaoke performance to encourage and cheer you as you perform.

I guess we can call this "Building Your Audience"

This way if you get nervous about the strange faces in the room you can look to your friends to help keep calm.

Be a good audience Member

Lastly, choosing a good audience means being a good audience. Cheer others when they sing and compliment them one on one, if possible. By doing this you're building a good audience which you are a part of, and that way you get good vibes and support for each person's singing.

CHAPTER 5

STEP #3: REHEARSE YOUR SONGS

Prepare Yourself

You're better prepared when you prepare! I mean 'Rehearse.' And it doesn't have to be stressful.

There are some easy things you can do to ensure you rehearse better, and your rehearsals don't have to be long and painful. Well of course you've got to work at it, but it can be made a tad easier.

One thing you can do is hire the services of a vocal coach to help you with your voice or watch voice coaching videos on YouTube. There are tons of them, quite helpful and instructional too.

Don't forget the Lyrics

To help make rehearsals better, download songs and lyrics online. You want to be sure you're singing the right lyrics.

Listen to songs with your headphone and record yourself while you sing. This helps you get familiar with the lyrics of the song.

Sing in front of your mirror or video yourself while you sing.

Better yet, make use of karaoke apps like *The VoiceOnStage* app by *Star Maker*. I personally use this app and find it very helpful.

Start with a warm Up

Always start with a simple vocal warmup for about 10 minutes or so to help waken your vocal chords.

You can start your rehearsals with a simple "Lip bubble" warmup. This exercise reduces vocal tension. All you need do is relax your lips and jaw and just blow air out from your mouth, through the lips just like you would do when swimming under the water surface.

This action produces a vibration of your lips and you should try to keep the vibration light and regular. This should be repeated for some time, and you'll definitely notice a difference in how you sound.

Ask a Friend

Ask a friend or friends who are better at singing to sing with you and help you practice before you go out to sing karaoke. Better still, you could sing together on the day of the performance.

Extra Tip - Use your hairbrush or something as your mic as that's kind of like what you'd hold on that day. I use my body spray can.

Note: Your rehearsals can continue up until the day of your performance but don't push it. Have good enough rest prior to your performance.

CHAPTER 6

STEP #4: DRESS UP FOR THE SHOW

You want to look good at your performance. Your karaoke performance would probably be at night so you should go with a good outfit that's suitable for a night out.

Below are some DO's and DON'T's on what to wear for a karaoke night.

DO's

* Tees - T-shirts are a Do for a karaoke performance. You can dress it up with a jacket or blazer.

* Jeans - Jeans are a major YES for karaoke and they just scream "Cool." Definitely a Do.

* Shirts - I like checkered shirts. You could pair it with a blue jean and sneakers and you're good to go. Pick a good shirt, plain if you prefer and even roll up the sleeves to add a little more style to it.

* Jackets and Blazers - These also add more pizzazz to your look. Try a blazer and a T-shirt or top(for ladies) with a nice neck chain.

* Sneakers - Everyone looks good in sneakers. Just rock it!

* Heels - Ladies, if you're comfortable rocking that stage in heels, go for it. Slay like a "Gladiator in heels" if you know what I mean. ;)

* Hats - Hats are an accessory that just make you look cool without even trying so hard. A Panama or Fedora hat would be a nice pick.

* Party Dress - A simple short party dress for ladies isn't a bad idea but I wouldn't really recommend it. However, it does make our DO list.

DON'T's

* Ball Gowns and Tuxes - No! No! No! It's karaoke, not a "Wedding Party" That's just it. No!

* Corsages and Tiaras - Unless you're *MBGN* queen (which still doesn't count much) please steer clear of these. Again, it's karaoke.

* Face Masks and costume-party-type dresses and accessories - Just NO!

Look smart for a night out. Don't be a drag and don't look like one.Just look good and Rock! No dulling!

PART THREE

THE STEPS - YOUR PERFORMANCE

CHAPTER 7

STEP #5: RELAX

While being nervous can be a good sign,it's not so good while you're singing.

You want to be in control and more relaxed while singing, and by relaxing I mean, calm yourself. Try to relax those nerves.

Have something Light

What you eat doesn't necessarily affect your vocal cords, but for optimum performance, you should eat at least 2 hours to your karaoke performance to make the most of it.

You could have something light prior to the performance if you're really hungry, but be sure to avoid certain foods like milk, that is if you have allergies, and no heavy foods whatsoever.

Note: What you eat does not come in contact your vocal folds. However, foods like Milk tend to increase phlegm in some persons but is not applicable to everybody.

Breathe

Before you take the stage, try calming yourself by doing some deep breathing exercises. Simply take long deep breaths. There are several breathing variations you can try too. This should get you relaxed.

You could also do some vocal warmups like the lip bubble we talked about earlier. Well, maybe not out in the open, so people don't start asking questions. Lol!

Cheer Others

Remember what we said earlier about choosing the right audience by being the right audience? Well, now would be a good time to be the right audience and cheer someone else as they perform.

Stay Connected

Relax! Don't take yourself too seriously. If you're naturally reserved like myself, go out of your way to make a friend or two. Strike up a conversation with someone you don't know. You are here to have fun not kill the fun. Connect!

Extra Tip - Another way to calm yourself is by closing your eyes and saying the alphabets backwards from Z to A.

This takes your mind off the nerves and gets your attention on trying to read backwards, and you might even make a few mistakes and have a good laugh at yourself while doing this. It'd sure help you relax.

CHAPTER 8

STEP #6: TAKE THE STAGE

Sound Check 1, 2! You feel goosebumps all over. You just want to do your best. Friends cheering! Spotlight's on you! What you gonna do?

Be Brave

Walk up that stage. Be Brave! Be bold and courageous, even if you feel like the dog, Courage from the cartoon series "Courage The Cowardly Dog" who in the face of danger, being terrified, faces his fears and saves the day.

It's like they say, "The Show Must Go On" and Go On it must. You can and must give your best even when it may not be convenient for you, or good enough for others. Just give it your best.

Lighten Up

Before you start singing, you can introduce yourself. Probably as you mount the stage, look around the room. Look at the faces of your audience. Smile to lighten up a bit. Compliment someone's shirt or something while on stage.

I wouldn't really recommend jokes but if your audience can handle a good joke, and you're sure it's a good one, I say let them have it, just to ease the tension and lighten up the room before you sing.

After all, it's only Karaoke.But then again, don't get carried away. Don't forget why you're there - to Sing.

Make eye Contact

While singing on stage, try to make eye contact. Making eye contact with members of the audience exudes confidence and draws your audience into your song.

Sure there are moments when you close your eyes and you just feel the lyrics of the song. You can't help it.

I do close my eyes when singing, but there are times I must open them to look at my audience. But keeping eye contact while singing can be tough, with all kinds of faces staring at you.

That just reminds me of a line from an old Nigerian song back in the day -"Face Fear Face" Familiar with it?

Well, that's a song in a different book, but there are ways to keep you looking in charge while singing, even if you're really not.

Tips on making eye Contact

Here are a few things to help keep you in charge of your performance:

1. Looking at different corners of the room to carry everyone along in your song is one way to go about it.

2. Look at the familiar faces in the crowd like friends or family. If you're doing a duet with a friend or family member, better. That way you can be more relaxed.

3. If there are no familiar faces to give you some encouragement, look at the screen if there is one. At least for the time being.

4. You can also look a little above the heads of your audience members to make it appear like you're looking at them. This works quite well.

You don't need to close your eyes to take away the tension. Not like there's anything wrong in that, but try these and see how much better it is, and with time, even while singing, the boldness to look folks in the eye will shine through.

CHAPTER 9

STEP #7: ENJOY YOURSELF

Smile

Don't forget to enjoy yourself while singing. Smile, if the song you're singing calls for it. Jollificate!

After all that's why you came; to have a good time. Enjoy yourself while singing, that way others would really enjoy you.

Get into the Song

Mean what you're singing about. Get into your song and feel the words and your audience will feel you.

If you miss a few notes, don't worry so much about it. Just get back on track.

Have fun and say "Thank You"

The most important thing is to have fun singing. To be relaxed while singing. Sing and enjoy your singing and also don't forget to smile andsay "Thank You."

Appreciate your audience for listening to your song and take a bow.

And if there's no round of applause or standing ovation, come on! It's karaoke and you gave it a shot. Just have fun and connect.

It's that **EASY**, you see!

So yeah, go ahead. Break A Leg! ;)

PART FOUR
YOUR JOURNEY

CHAPTER 10

READY TO SING?

First of all, congratulations! You took that bold STEP but, that you took the step doesn't make your success automatic.

You just keep working at it and making those positive connections, and you'll keep on climbing.

If you follow the steps laid out in this book, you're sure to be better at singing karaoke this weekend and it just might be the start of your singing career.

I have mentioned that several times now

Okay, I know you might be thinking "not so fast Bobee, I'm still new to this." Well, we were all newbies at some point. Everyone started off somewhere and decided to keep getting better.

Would you like to get better at singing, get access to some really helpful content on singing and connect with other singers? Then I encourage you to be a part of a singing group in church, in your school, a band, and even online.

There are several groups on Facebook to help singers with useful content. You can also JOIN our community on Facebook. JOIN our Facebook Group @TheSingdom.

Choose to believe in yourself and your abilities. Be confident. You have a voice too. But it's up to you to take action, go out there, connect, and sing like the star that you are.

You can reach me at bobeeadimibe@gmail.com for your thoughts on this book and suggestions as to what other topic you would like to learn about.

It's your time to shine.

Shine!

~Bobee Adimibe

Glossary

Karaoke box - a room, usually more than one, containing karaoke equipment, rented for certain time periods.

MBGN Queen- Most Beautiful Girl Nigeria Pageant is the biggest beauty queenpageant in Nigeria.

NYSC - National Youth Service Corps, which is kind of one year of military service in the US.

Vocal range- havingtodowithoctavebracketwi thinwhichyoucansing

Printed in Great Britain
by Amazon

53914301R00030